The Wise Woman

The Archetype of Knowledge and Wisdom

Books by the Author

Non-Fiction

Archetypes:

  Archetypes, unmasking your true self (Possumwood, 2012)

  The Knight the archetype of quest (Possumwood 2017)

  The Queen the archetype of leadership (Possumwood 2017)

  The Princess the archetype of privilege (Possumwood 2019)

  The King the archetype of command (Possumwood 2020)

  The Prince the archetype of charm (Possumwood 2020)

  The Priestess the archetype of feminine guidance (Possumwood 2020)

  The Court Jester the archetype of wit and humour (Possumwood 2020)

  The Wise Woman the archetype of knowledge and wisdom (Possumwood 2020)

Other:

  Self-Esteem Matters (Possumwood, 2015)

  Fear Not (Possumwood, 2018)

  Decoding the Afterlife (Possumwood 2016)

Fiction

Tilly and the Magic Potion (Possumwood, 2013)

Charlie the Cheeky Spider (Possumwood, 2017)

Fantastic Adventures what would YOU do? (Possumwood, 2020)

Contact the Author

Email: *briandale1@bigpond.com*

Web: *briandale.com.au*

      possumwoodpublishing.com

The Wise Woman

The Archetype of Knowledge and Wisdom

Brian Dale

Illustrations by Lily Loy and Cas Harders

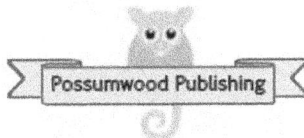

Possumwood Publishing

Possumwood Publishing
5 Possumwood Place, Mullumbimby, NSW 2482 Australia
possumwoodpublishing@gmail.com

First published in 2020
Copyright © Brian Dale, 2020

Dale, Brian Richard
The Wise Woman
Archetypes
Personality traits
Psychology
Spirituality

Illustrations by Lily Loy and Cas Harders
Cover illustration by Cas Harders
Editing and typesetting by Jan Dale
Cover design by Jan Dale

Printed by Kindle Direct Publishing, an Amazon.com Company
Published by Possumwood Publishing

Dedication

This book is dedicated to Robyn Faye, my life-time friend, wife and inspiration.

She is truly the Wise Woman

Table of Contents

The Wise Woman

How to harness your wisdom, increase your knowledge, use your psychic abilities with confidence, assist those who come to you for advice, maintain honesty and discretion, establish and grow your status within the community and experience personal growth to strengthen your link with the spiritual and the physical.

Yes! You are the Wise Woman

You understand that you are the Wise Woman because you have knowledge, understanding and wisdom that are deep within your persona. You understand feminine issues. You provide family and community leadership. You are the link between the physical and the spiritual dimensions. Others constantly seek your advice because they recognize your wisdom, your knowledge and your discretion. Others acknowledge the Wise Woman within you and you should do the same, no matter your age. Yes, the Wise Woman, Crone or Sage grows into her power and wisdom. However, you have had these qualities from a very young age. Understand who you are and never deny the qualities you possess and what gifts you have to share with others. You are the Wise Woman.

Are you ready to harness your wisdom?

Wisdom is learnt through experience. Wisdom is also intuitive. It is time to acknowledge that you are wise. The time to focus on that wisdom is now. Are you ready? Of course you are, because you are reading these words. These words are for you. Take up the challenge. Understand that an important part of you is the Wise Woman. Use your intuition with confidence and self-assuredness. Life experiences enhance your wisdom while belief and practice expand your intuitive nature. You are ready.

For, you are the Wise Woman

Are you ready to increase your knowledge?

Of course you are, for you have been on this path for a very long time. You have always asked questions and sought knowledge. You have always possessed a library full of material that assists your knowledge. You have always listened to people and taken on the information that was relevant to you and to others that come to you for advice. You have always been the person within your group that others would come to for consultation. You have always been interested in family, femininity, children, child birth, education, raising children, medical practices, what is natural and what is manufactured, social justice, psychological well-being, spiritual issues and the connectedness of all things.

You are the Wise Woman

Are you willing to assist those who come to you for advice?

This is a rhetorical question because you have been doing this from a very young age. Even when you were in primary or elementary school, your friends would come seeking your advice. They recognised your intuitive wisdom, your impartiality and your ability to give fair advice without any strings attached. This process grew throughout your teenage years when there were a whole range of identity and social issues to deal with. As you grew into adulthood, there were adult issues to deal with. Your friends may have changed but you are the constant. You are the encyclopaedia or the search engine for personal, social and spiritual advice.

You have always been, and always are, the Wise Woman.

How do you establish and maintain your status within the family and community?

How do you assist all those who seek your advice?

The answer lies in understanding, trust and practice.

Understand who you are.

Trust in your ability and wisdom.

Practice your skills on a regular basis.

How do we deal with the energy of the Wise Woman and provide an understanding into their nature?

Recognition of the Wise Woman Archetype

You are the Wise Woman. You have an inherent understanding of the spiritual, social and biological aspects of humanity. As you grow in confidence with your wisdom and understanding, you grow in your statue as the Wise Woman.

As you begin to understand your talents and hone your skills, you gain a perspective into your strengths. You also follow a vocational pathway that best utilizes your knowledge and skills.

You are a Wise Woman.

Recognize the Wise Woman archetype.

Use the archetypal energy for personal development, advice to family and friends and for community leadership and counselling.

How do we deal with the Wise Woman and recognize the accompanying archetypal energy?

Wise Women:

- have an innate knowledge of the feminine
- are sought after by their peers, especially women, for advice
- are the trusted source of information regarding family, relationships, children, childbirth, medical advice and spirituality
- possess a library of non-fiction material
- have access to sources of information or individuals who have knowledge about feminine issues
- take on responsibilities of social leadership
- provide an alternative voice on issues of femininity, health, social inclusion, family, spirituality to that offered by the mainstream social sources
- are discreet in their discussions with others
- grow in wisdom and knowledge with age and experience

Do you have an understanding of the Wise Woman energy and personality traits?

Can you recognize those aspects of you that have always been with you?

Are you aware of the occasions when you have been called upon or when you have incidentally used the knowledge and wisdom of the Wise Woman?

Have you accepted the responsibility of the Wise Woman?

Good! Then let us proceed.

The Wise Woman Archetype

How to:

❖ harness your wisdom

❖ increase your knowledge

❖ use your psychic abilities with confidence

❖ assist those who come to you for advice

❖ maintain honesty and discretion

❖ establish and grow your status within the community

❖ experience personal growth to strengthen your link with the spiritual and the physical

❧ Acceptance ❧

As Wise Women mature, they grow in wisdom and knowledge. They begin to understand the role they play in society and in their social group. They begin to accept their position and the responsibility that goes with it.

All archetypes are a part of our personality from our birth to our death. Because of their youth and lack of life experiences, children with the Wise Woman archetype have a much vaguer understanding of this aspect of their personality than other aspects. For example, as a young girl, it is a lot easier to acknowledge and identify with the traits of a Princess rather than those of the Wise Woman. The characteristics of the Princess are simpler and far less demanding than those of the Wise Woman.

It is for this reason of complexity that girls and young woman find it a challenge to accept the responsibilities and identification of the Wise Woman energy.

A major task for the individual with the Wise Woman archetype is to accept that part of their personality. There has to be willingness and an understanding of who they truly are, of the rights and responsibilities that go with the role of Wise Woman. Once this has been accepted, the Wise Woman has made the first step in claiming her power.

❧ Humility ❧

One of the greatest assets of the Wise Woman is humility. This is also one of the reasons the Wise Woman denies her wisdom, plays down her leadership role and her ability to assist others. The Wise Woman is there to serve family, friends and the community. The family, tribe or peer group depend upon the Wise Woman for advice on a whole range of social issues. Honest social interaction, positive relationships and individual personal growth are important to the health and cohesion of all societies and peer groups and the role of the Wise Woman is paramount.

It is therefore beneficial that the Wise Woman take on her role with humility. Advice is to be given from a position of equality and not from a position of superiority or self-glorification. It is important the Wise Woman never takes on the position of the righteous and all-knowing guru. The humble Wise Woman conducts her affairs with discretion and inner peace. There is no need for the Wise Woman to boast or be placed upon a pedestal. The positive archetypal Wise Woman has that inner knowing about her sense of duty and service. They understand that each individual can take pride in her work and her achievements and this can be done with humility and unpretentiousness.

❧ Responsibility ❧

As the Wise Woman matures and recognizes her role in society, her involvement and actions demand a greater level of responsibility.

As a young girl or teenager, the individual with the Wise Woman archetype is often thrown into the role of relationship advisor. Her role is to sort out any conflicts within the peer group, give advice on social protocols, provide emotional support to those in distress and offer counselling on personal matters.

There are questions about physical development. Friends and acquaintances approach the young Wise Woman with questions about their physical development and menstruation cycle. They know and understand the Wise Woman has the knowledge and is bound to answer with honesty. They realize that their personal information is safe with the Wise Woman. After all, the Wise Woman and the Detective archetypes are the epitome of discretion.

As a young woman, the issues presented to the Wise Woman become greater in number and in complexity. Relationships, gender identification, sex, childbirth, raising children, vocational guidance, health issues, addictions, personal well-being, religion and spiritual beliefs may all become part of the brief of the Wise Woman.

As life's joys and challenges are experienced at a personal level and others seek her advice for a wider range of subjects, the knowledge and wisdom of the Wise Woman increases. The question becomes, "What do I do with this knowledge and with the individuals that come to me for advice?" It is up to the individual Wise Woman to take up the challenge. Do they take up a leadership role and begin teaching or organize group programs? Is there a specialized field that they can contribute to in a purposeful and meaningful way? Do they leave the comfort of their own home, family and society and travel to places or societies that need and would benefit from her expertise? Responsibility often demands sacrifice. It is up to the individual Wise Woman to decide where their responsibility lies and how much they are willing to challenge themselves.

⊰ Custodian ⊱

The Wise Woman is the custodian of social traditions. Information that is handed down from generation to generation is entrusted to the Wise Woman. This individual is acknowledged for her wisdom and discretion.

Many of the customs and traditions that are the domain of the Wise Woman revolve around women and the feminine spirit. In the tribal tradition it was the Wise Woman or elders who passed on the stories to their children, advised and assisted with childbirth and child rearing. They possessed knowledge of plants and herbs and administered medicinal remedies. They supervised the emotional and psychological well-being of the tribe and became their spiritual guide and advisor.

All these traditions and all this knowledge is still the domain of the modern Wise Woman. The area that now places greater demands on the Wise Woman is in spiritual leadership. Over time, religions stole many of the spiritual traditions and ways of the tribe. Religions and their organizational structure gave power, custodianship and leadership to men. Men became the dominant force in spiritual and religious matters. The role of the Wise Woman was constricted. However, with the recognition of equal rights and opportunities for women, especially in modern and civil societies, religions have failed to keep pace with this progress. Women are still seeking spiritual guidance, not through religion or the church but through personal and small group experiences. This situation places demands on, and presents opportunities to, the Wise Woman. The need is there. Take up the challenge and let it be part of your spiritual journey.

◄§ Personal Growth ᶤ

The Wise Woman is attuned to personal growth. There are archetypal energies that live very much in the physical. These include archetypes such as the Banker, Servant, Slave, Adventurer, Martyr, Athlete, Warrior and Engineer. The energy of these archetypes is designed to assist the individual through the physical chores, duties, and pleasures of daily living. These individuals are content to immerse themselves in the physical plane and sensory experiences.

There are also archetypal energies that spend a great deal of their focus on spiritual evolvement. These include archetypes such as the Mystic, Priestess, Priest, Monk, Nun and Goddess. The energy of these archetypes is for spiritual connection and individual evolvement. They are looking for personal growth in both their spiritual knowledge and wisdom and the positive expression of their humanity. The Wise Woman is one of these archetypes.

The Wise Woman has a natural curiosity and willingness to learn, understand and evolve. She has a basic desire to ask questions, to expand her knowledge, to engage with a deeper spiritual connection and to ensure her advice is relevant and meets the needs of those seeking help. This is one of the reasons the Wise Woman has an expanding library of non-fiction books. It also explains why the Wise Woman participates in workshops and learning experiences. There is this basic desire to know and experience more, to grow personally and to become more aware of matters close to her heart.

As knowledge and experience increase, so does wisdom. The Wise Woman matures into their power. This is a process. It takes place at a rate that is acceptable to the individual Wise Woman and the circle of peers. It is a process that is neither rushed nor forced. It is also a process that cannot be denied.

When the Wise Woman uses the positive energy of the archetype, she seeks opportunities for growth. She attends events and seminars. She is willing to assist those who seek her advice. She specializes and hones her skills in a specific area such as childbirth or psychology. She takes on responsibilities and positions of leadership. She challenges the status quo. She accepts her strengths and challenges herself to be better. She enjoys the process of personal growth and journeys enthusiastically on life's pathway.

◆ Leadership ◆

The Wise Woman is a leader. The energy of the Wise Woman is not like other leadership energies. Individuals with the King, Queen, Statesperson, Politician, Indulged Child, Shaman and Advocate are keen to stamp their authority on situations, people or events. They revel in the power of leadership. However, there are other archetypal energies that take on leadership roles with more reluctance. The Wise Woman is one of those archetypal energies.

Assisting a friend through an emotional crisis is a challenge in leadership. The situation may be a relationship break-up, the death of a family member or close friend or helping the individual escape from, and deal with, serious abuse. This may be a one-on-one situation but the Wise Woman is called upon to be the leader and use her knowledge and wisdom to deal with a variety of challenges.

Leadership varies from situation to situation, especially for the Wise Woman. There are occasions when it is a personal one-on-one situation. There are other occasions when the group is small in number and the responsibilities of leadership may not be arduous. However, there are occasions when the group may be large in number, the challenges immense and the responsibilities for leadership far more demanding.

The key is for the Wise Woman to understand that she has the knowledge and wisdom to deal with all manner of crises. It is a matter of confidence and trust. When the Wise Woman has confidence in her knowledge and trust in the process, everything can be dealt with clarity and purpose.

As the Wise Woman grows in confidence and trust, she is more content to take on greater leadership responsibilities. Conducting workshops, facilitating special interest groups, taking up a position of advocacy or being elected as a group representative are situations where the Wise Woman is thrust into leadership and responsibility.

The decision and timing to take on leadership roles is up to the individual Wise Woman. She knows when she is ready. If there is still reluctance, a critical occasion inevitably arises. The tribe knows who the Wise Woman is and the tribe knows when assistance and leadership are required.

11

⤙ Social Advisor ⤚

The Wise Woman is the lynchpin of social cohesion. Peacemaking, negotiation and communication skills are learnt at a very young age. These skills are developed with maturity, exposure to a wide range of life experiences and confronting and dealing with challenges presented by others to the Wise Woman.

The whole range of social interaction is likely to become the domain of the Wise Woman. There are discussions about the choice of partners, how to improve relationships or deal with issues of disagreement, the role of each partner within a relationship, physical and sexual cohesion, economic priorities and decisions (income, spending, saving), bringing children into the relationship, agreed parenting techniques, finding time and attention for both children and partner and other issues that deal with personal wellbeing.

As well as dealing with individual cases and relationships, the Wise Woman may be cast in the role of social leader. This is especially prevalent through pre-teens and teenage years. The peer group is often looking to leadership and the Wise Woman becomes a magnet for others still finding their way into adulthood and personal identity.

There are still occasions when the tribal elder has the responsibility to lead ritual and ceremony. This is often the domain of the Shaman and the Priestess. The Shaman deals with the masculine energy and rituals while the Priestess has the duty with the feminine energy and rituals. Often the roles of the Priestess and the Wise Woman are identical. Often the energies of both archetypes are within the one individual. It is then up to the Wise Woman to be the elder and conduct ceremonies that introduce young females into the world of social exposure and maturity.

❧ Health and Wellbeing ❧

The Wise Woman has the knowledge and understanding about her personal health and wellbeing. She also is a wealth of information and a reliable source of advice for others who come to her. Her knowledge and understanding on health is multi-faceted. The Wise Woman deals with physical health, mental and psychological wellbeing and spiritual connection. Much of this knowledge comes from an intuitive base. If the Wise Woman needs further confirmation, she accesses the pages of books in her library.

Much of the knowledge the Wise Woman has at her disposal is ancient wisdom. She may be a channel for that wisdom. She may come upon that wisdom via her intuition. Therefore, a great deal of her advice concerns natural remedies. It may include herbal remedies and natural medicines, aromatherapy, yoga, massage and other such treatments. It is about the food we eat. It is about what is healthy for our body and what is needed by our body. It is about the environment we live in. It is about the type of drugs and poisons we put into our system. It is about our connection to spirit. It is about harnessing the power of the mind. It is about mental health and psychological wellbeing, as well as physical health.

The Wise Woman has an understanding of modern medicine. She understands the wonders that modern medicine delivers. She also understands the misuse of modern medicine and the harm it inflicts upon the individual. There is often the dilemma of combining modern medicine with ancient medical wisdom. This brings in the Wise Woman's ability of discernment. The individual seeking her advice may be left with a combination of modern and ancient medicine. This combination may be more beneficial than one singular approach.

The Wise Woman understands the concept of holistic health and wellbeing. She is interested in a holistic approach. She understands that health is not delivered by 'the magic bullet' approach. Health is attained and maintained by conscious living and good habits. It is the Wise Woman's sense of duty that advice given to others is individual, relevant and on-going.

The sense of individual responsibility and the development of a personal relationship are important. The health of any one individual is a partnership between the client and the practitioner.

The Wise Woman understands this and puts this knowledge into practice. The Wise Woman understands her role of advisor. If the individual wants to attain and maintain optimum health, then it is up to them. The Wise Woman cannot do it for them. The Wise Woman is there to advise, encourage and monitor. For all of that, the Wise Woman's personality traits are ideal.

You are the Wise Woman. Understand that you have ancient and recent knowledge in regards to health and wellbeing. As always, the key is to begin with your personal health. When you are a fine example of physical, emotional and psychological wellbeing, you are in a strong position to advise others.

৯৯ Childbirth and Raising Children ৯৯

As the Wise Woman grows and matures into adulthood, the advice that others seek changes in nature. The questions of relationships, femininity and sexuality, although still important, give way to the subject of childbirth and rearing of children.

The Wise Woman may, or may not, have children of her own. Having your own children does give a first-hand knowledge and understanding of the process of childbirth and the stages that children go through. However, the Wise Woman is an expert at channelling. Information and advice that is sought is often channelled and passed on publicly via a group gathering or privately to an individual.

Having a child is a natural moment in the continuity of womanhood. Modern advancements in health and medicine have seen the wonders of making a difficult and life-threatening birth into a more simple procedure.

On the other hand, the demands of health authorities have added layers of complexities to a natural event. Governments, doctors and hospitals add their layer of bureaucracy to the birthing process. There are now more decisions to be made and more details to consider than in previous times.

This is where the Wise Woman plays her role. She has the knowledge to impart and the understanding that each of us is different. To make childbirth the most positive and rewarding experience, the desires of the mother-to-be are crucial and should always be a priority. Consideration of both the baby and mother's needs are linked. Independent advice is to be welcomed. This is why so many mid-wives have the Wise Woman archetype. It is their natural vocation.

Childbirth, of course, is just the beginning of parenthood. Throughout a child's life there are a multitude of decisions to be made. There is no manual to raising a child. The Wise Woman has the knowledge and the connection to assist with the child-rearing process. This is not to suggest that the Wise Woman takes over the process. That is always the responsibility of the parents. However, Wise Women are the source of knowledge, be they the mother, grandmother, aunt, friend or community worker.

By using the positive energy of this archetype, the Wise Woman gives generously. She is not reliant upon her attitudes or values but is always independent to these.

As the Wise Woman, you have a natural instinct in assisting new mothers through the pre-natal and ante-natal processes. If you have a Mother archetype as well, that gives you extra knowledge and wisdom to share. Use your archetypal energy to care and assist others. As the Wise Woman, you have an abundance of wisdom to guide and advise others who may be fearful and not as knowledgeable. That is the calling for the Wise Woman.

❧ Spiritual Link ❧

Spirituality is the personal link between an individual and the Divine. If you prefer to use the word God, Spirit or any other then you are free to do so. It is all the same energy.

The key with the Wise Woman energy is to provide that link between the individual and the Divine. Spirituality is not the same as religion. A religion has taken certain aspects of the overall spiritual existence and taught them as dogma to a selective band. Religion has exclusivity and a hierarchy. Spirituality is not exclusive and has no hierarchy. Spirituality is inclusive. All energy, all life is connected to the God-force or Divine energy. Spirituality is a state of contented and serene existence. It is a state of peace, love and surrender.

The Wise Woman never preaches or tells an individual what to believe in or how to live their life. The Wise Woman is a conduit. She connects the individual with the Divine. She answers questions. She may suggest directions but leaves all choice to the individual.

The Wise Woman is aware of her personal spirituality. She understands her attachment with the Divine. She understands her role as the conduit. She always has that ability to channel spiritual information to those who seek spiritual guidance and truth. That is the nature and archetypal energy of the Wise Woman.

Rejoice in your spiritual essence. There are only a few archetypes that have the energetic ability to tap into their personal spirituality and to provide a spiritual link to assist others. You are the Wise Woman who has knowledge and wisdom. Use those talents well and use them often.

You are the Wise Woman.

Be confident of your ability and trust in the knowledge and wisdom that comes to you and through you. That is the Divine gift to be shared with others. That is the purpose of the Wise Woman.

Understand:

- ❖ how to harness your wisdom
- ❖ increase your knowledge
- ❖ use your psychic abilities with confidence
- ❖ assist those who come to you for advice,
- ❖ maintain honesty and discretion,
- ❖ establish and grow your status within the community
- ❖ experience personal growth to strengthen your link with the spiritual and the physical.

Complementary Relationship Archetypes

As you are the Wise Woman, it is to your benefit to understand other archetypes that complement this energy. Some of these archetypes may be your personal archetypes as well as the Wise Woman. Also, there are individuals with these archetypes who are drawn to you and who work well with your energy. Individuals who work co-operatively and productively empower themselves and give strength to the group dynamic. It is the function of the Wise Woman to use their knowledge and wisdom in harnessing these archetypal powers for the benefit of all within their field of influence.

✍ Priestess ✍

The Priestess and the Wise Woman have very similar, energies, characteristics and personality traits. Both have a knowing and understanding of spiritual, feminine and relationship issues. Both are connected to their tribe. Remember the tribe is never a static group of people. Unlike in ancient times, the tribe in modern societies is a fluid group of like-minded or enquiring individuals who enter the tribe then leave when they are called elsewhere.

The key difference between the Wise Woman and the Priestess is with ritual. The Priestess is the female of the tribe who conducts ceremonies. She always has an altar adorned with crystals, feathers, runes, symbolic ornaments and objects. She adorns herself with symbolic clothing, ornaments and tattoos. She leads the tribe in spiritual and ceremonial rituals such as meditation, yoga, initiations and the like.

The Wise Woman leads a more covert life. She rarely advertises who she is and the knowledge and wisdom she possesses. The individuals who seek this knowledge and wisdom are attracted to the calm and simple energy of the Wise Woman. Individuals who approach the Wise Woman are generally looking for advice and guidance rather than ceremony and ritual. They prefer consultation rather than overt participation. This requirement is to be respected and often it is the energy of the Wise Woman that is more suited. As the client grows in confidence and awareness, their needs may gravitate more to the energy of the Priestess.

It is common for an individual to have both Wise Woman and Priestess archetypes. When the Wise Woman combines her energy with the energy of the Priestess, it is a powerful combination. This energetic combination presents the best in advice, guidance, ceremony and ritual. The individual and the tribe benefit greatly when surrounded by these energies.

◦§ Guide ҂◦

The positive archetypal energy or personality traits of the Guide are similar in nature to the positive archetypal energy of the Wise Woman. Both archetypes allow the individual to channel relevant information. Both archetypes encourage the individual to advise and give information devoid of personal bias and interference. Both archetypes encourage information to be given freely and without attachment as to whether the information is taken up or discarded. Both archetypes have an understanding that feedback is rarely forthcoming and not required. The confidence in one's ability is the essence of these archetypes.

Both the Wise Woman and the Guide lead by example. The archetype of the Wise Woman is more common in this era of human development. This is the case because of the expansion of population, knowledge and opportunity. There is so much to know. There are so many issues confronting humanity. In many countries and societies, the power of organized religions has diminished. Popular leadership is full of slogans and clichés. People are looking for deeper knowledge, advice and awareness.

The energy of the Wise Woman is found in individuals in many walks of life. The Wise Woman energy is devoted to our physical, emotional and psychological wellbeing as well as our spiritual understanding and evolvement.

The Guide energy, in essence, is devoted to the more spiritual aspect. It is a quiet energy. The individual with the Guide archetype rarely advertises their energy. They go about their daily life with calmness, purpose and awareness of their sacred and spiritual essence.

✂ Seeker ✄

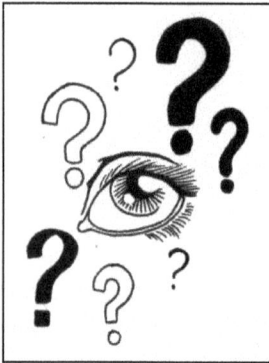

The individual with the Seeker archetype is continually asking questions and looking for the answers. The personality traits or positive energies of the Seeker serve the Wise Woman well. The Wise Woman also looks for the answers, especially on matters of spirituality, femininity and relationships. This is one of the reasons the Wise Woman has a library full of books, relevant to her expertise.

The key for the Seeker and the Wise Woman is to direct their curiosity and seeking into order and relevance. It is easy for all individuals to wander into areas of irrelevance or distraction. Once the Wise Woman establishes her priorities and follows her passion, she is able to harness the positive energies of both archetypes and use those energies with purpose and direction.

If you have both Wise Woman and Seeker archetypes, you have the knowledge, wisdom and the means to deal will all manner of questions and requests. If your friends or companions have the Seeker archetype, they are an important mechanism to activate your psychic abilities and inspire you to the time-honoured traditional role of the Sage. The Wise Woman is a seeker. They are a seeker for knowledge and truth. Always remember that you, the Wise Woman, have all you ever need to know within your inner self. That is the nature and wisdom of the Wise Woman.

⊰ Philosopher ⊱

The Philosopher is aligned with the Seeker in that both archetypal energies are concerned with asking questions and finding the answers. The difference lies in the manner of the questions and the process of answering those questions.

The Philosopher is concerned with deep and meaningful questions regarding our spiritual and physical existence, our purpose, the Afterlife, how our society is structured and social cohesion. The Seeker is concerned with all manner of questions and has the desire to find the answers as quickly as possible, whereas the Philosopher is more concerned with the thinking process and consideration of all possible answers or solutions.

The Philosopher energy is generally a more relevant energy to the Wise Woman than the Seeker energy. The Philosopher energy is more concerned with spiritual and social issues which are usually relevant to the matters that are presented to the Wise Woman. The Wise Woman deals with issues regarding our spiritual purpose and essence. She is constantly faced with questions regarding self-esteem, worthiness and feminine empowerment. Personal relationships and social interaction are subjects of specialty for the Wise Woman. She has been dealing with these issues from the age of a young child. All of these topics are the types of issues, about which, the friends or acquaintances of the Wise Woman seek her advice.

When the Wise Woman surrounds herself with the energy of the Philosopher and her own archetypal energy of the Wise Woman, she is a source of deep and powerful wisdom. It is important to use this knowledge and wisdom to the benefit of all. It is equally important to understand the benefits of action. The Philosopher finds it easy and comfortable to be drawn into the thinking process. Too much time in thinking is likely to inhibit the actions of the Wise Woman. When leadership is required, action is needed and the thinking process should take second place. It is important for the Wise Woman to understand the connection between thinking and action. Thinking and consideration may come first, but action must follow and follow with speed and relevance.

❧ Mother ☙

The combination of the Mother and Wise Woman archetypes creates an amazing caring, nurturing and guiding energy. It generates both spiritual and physical knowledge and wisdom.

The woman who has children of her own may not necessarily have a Mother archetype. Many mothers raise their children with a different archetypal energy. The Wise Woman archetype is commonly chosen and used in these situations. It is the guidance, advice and delicate communication of the Wise Woman who raises positive and balanced children.

When both Mother and Wise Woman energies combine, both the physical and spiritual development of the child is enhanced. The caring and nurturing energy of the positive Mother archetype is supreme in dealing with the physical, emotional and psychological needs of the child. Then, with the spiritual and feminine energy of the positive Wise Woman, there is the link to both the child's spiritual aspect and their physicality.

The Wise Woman is especially knowledgeable in raising children. She has inherent understanding and wisdom in regards to the nature of children. She instinctively knows when the child requires discipline, explanation or tender, loving care.

The Wise Woman has effective communication skills. She communicates with brevity, relevance and clarity. This suits children, whose focus and understanding is limited. Long, cluttered directions or messages are confusing and a waste of time and energy. Yes, the Mother and Wise Woman archetypes make a great combination.

The other benefit for the Wise Woman who undertakes the role of motherhood is the fact that she has been dealing with relationships for most of her life. This gives her knowledge, wisdom and experience when dealing with the relationship she has with her child or children. It also gives her wisdom when intervention is needed within family relationships.

❧ Mentor ❧

The Mentor archetype is a teaching archetype. The Mentor archetype belongs to the individual who works with a single individual or small group. It is very much like the relationship between the master and the apprentice.

The Wise Woman archetype has the personality traits of the teacher. Usually this is a one-to-one relationship. This is the combination of the Mentor and Wise Woman energies. Generally, later in life, when the individual with the Wise Woman archetype has learnt to trust her abilities and has had a variety of life experiences, she then takes on the role of tribal or community leader. This step broadens her teaching archetypal energy from a Mentor to a Teacher. This is to be commended, although the Wise Woman is generally content to invest her time and knowledge with a single individual and use her Mentor energy.

One of the positive actions of the Wise Woman is to take on an apprentice. This is often the case in matters of psychic and spiritual development. One understands the role of the Wise Woman as a Mentor, as psychic ability and spiritual connection is a truly personal experience.

❧ Disciple ❧

The Wise Woman is the female who has the knowledge and the wisdom to advise and assist others within her tribe or group, especially other females. The Disciple is the archetype with the energy and personality traits that encourages a sense of belonging and group involvement. In other words, the individuals with the Disciple archetype align themselves with membership of the tribe.

The energy of the Disciple is about loyalty, belonging and putting the needs of the group ahead of the needs of each individual. These individuals are invaluable members of the Wise Woman's circle of friends, acquaintances or clients. They are the people who seek the advice of the Wise Woman. They are the friends, who gather in groups seeking spiritual knowledge, advice on health, relationships, raising children and similar topics. They are the friends, acquaintances and clients who attend seminars and workshops hosted or facilitated by the Wise Woman.

As many of the friends and clients of the Wise Woman have the Disciple archetype, it is an important for the Wise Woman to understand that energy. There are certain considerations for the Wise Woman to take into account.

Firstly, these people are the essence of her tribe or group. They are the friends and clients who support the Wise Woman in the expansion of her personal knowledge and influence. They build her reputation. They network and bring others into the tribe.

Secondly, while belonging to the group and showing loyalty to that group; the Disciple is also seeking advice and empowerment. At a personal level, the Disciple is looking for ways to change their lives. The positive energy of the Wise Woman understands this. Therefore, it is important that the advice given and the teachings of the Wise Woman are relevant to their clients.

Thirdly, the aim of empowering the individual with the Disciple archetype is to foster strength and independence. When this individual is ready to leave the tribe and move on to another phase of their life, the Wise Woman allows this to happen freely and with devotion. The Wise Woman has done her job and done it successfully.

↫ Carer ↬

Another archetypal energy associated with the Wise Woman is that of the Carer. Individuals with the Carer archetype look after and care for others. This is done without fuss or fanfare. This is done with composure and empathy. This is done with little recognition or recompense. These individuals are employed as nurses, child care workers, integration aides, disability facilitators and those who work in aged care and similar industries.

The individual with the Carer archetype is always given people to look after and care for. They generally do not actively seek out people to change or reform. They just naturally take on that type of employment or others seek out their caring and nurturing personalities.

This is often the case with the Wise Woman. She generally does not seek out others to assist and advise. It is more likely others come to her. Therefore, the nature of the Carer and the Wise Woman are similar in this regard.

The Wise Woman has the knowledge and wisdom to assist others. They have the ability to tune into the needs and energies of the people they care for. They have a soft, gentle nurturing nature which makes the Wise Woman an ideal carer. If you are elderly, frail, ill or disabled, you could do no better than to have a Wise Woman look after and care for you.

Healer

Another archetypal energy associated with the Wise Woman is the Healer. Successful Healers understand that healing is a partnership. It is a partnership between Healer and patient. The positive Wise Woman understands this concept as well.

Many Healers who follow a career path, or find their purpose, take on a position of expertise. The Wise Woman may do this. She becomes a specialized doctor or a nurse, a psychologist or a psychiatrist. She becomes a Reiki master or develops an expertise in similar fields. She becomes a chemist or herbalist. She follows her passion and her interests to excel in her chosen field.

The Wise Woman may stay true to her universal nature and involve herself in the many aspects of healing. The holistic approach is often the way of the Wise Woman. This is a likely scenario when the Wise Woman has family or takes up a vocation as a teacher or similar profession. It may also come to the fore by facilitating groups that meet for knowledge or healing. It is important to understand the Wise Woman has access to universal knowledge. They may decide to use that knowledge and wisdom to teach in a whole variety of ways. The energy of the Wise Woman is always present and always at the ready to educate, to assist and advise.

❧ Angel ❧

There are several archetypes that have a strong spiritual connection. Mystic, Goddess, Divine Child, Priestess, Angel and Wise Woman are some of these archetypes.

The Angel and the Wise Woman are similar in their spiritual connection. The two archetypes have similar energies or personality traits. Both energies are quiet and subtle in nature. The individual with the Wise Woman or Angel is empathetic and compassionate. They have respect for all living things and a great desire to see all life thrive and reach its full potential. Both the Wise Woman and the Angel have the energy and ability to tune into others and give advice that is honest, discerning and without any strings attached.

The words and actions of the positive Wise Woman and Angel energy are filled with love and compassion. There is never any judgement or criticism, only love and acceptance.

❧ Companion ❧

The energy of the Companion archetype is similar to the energy of the Disciple archetype. The personality traits of both archetypes encourage loyalty and the advancement of others. With the Disciple, it is the group dynamic that is important. With the Companion archetype, it is the individual the Companion supports who is important.

If the Wise Woman is surrounded by others who are loyal and keen for the advancement of the Wise Woman and the group, then harmony and influence flourish. Loyalty gives encouragement to the Wise Woman. It gives confirmation of her knowledge and ability to advise others with relevance and impartiality. It gives her personal confidence. It also gives her authority in her role to assist others.

It is important for the Wise Woman to understand her position of authority and leadership, especially when dealing with Companion energy. Others in the tribe or group look up to the Wise Woman, not only as a friend and advisor but also as a Guide. As with all positive Guide energy, the Wise Woman's task is to give advice with relevance and impartiality. When the advice is given, it is always the decision of the recipient to either accept or reject this advice. The positive energy of the Wise Woman insists there is no attachment to what is given. The individual with the Companion archetype must have the freedom to choose what is best for them.

It is important for the Wise Woman to honour her leadership status and to do so with humility. Positive leadership is never about control. Positive leadership is about bringing people together to inspire them to work on personal and common goals. The true leader assists others, as well as themselves, to achieve and pursue their life's purpose with joy and enthusiasm.

~ Networker ~

The energy of the Networker is another positive energy that is beneficial to the Wise Woman. The Networker energy brings others into the Wise Woman's sphere of influence. The Networker energy brings clients to the Wise Woman. This is important when the Wise Woman establishes a business, utilizing her knowledge and skills. There is nothing wrong with this process. Leading a spiritual life does not demand the psychic or knowledgeable individual give their skills freely. Receiving and accepting recompense for your skill is perfectly acceptable in any walk of life.

The other important role of the Networker is to bring influential people to the Wise Woman. This promotes the Wise Woman, not just at a personal level, but also at a social level. With positive promotion, the Wise Woman gains in reputation and confidence. It also brings into the fold and sphere of influence, others who have been seeking the appropriate advice or consultative person. This is a win-win situation for all concerned.

Employment ~ Vocation

⚶ Education and Teaching ⚵

The individual with the Wise Woman archetype is born to teach. She has the knowledge and the wisdom others seek. She has the ability to give advice with relevance and impartiality. She has the ability to guide and inspire. She has the understanding to allow others to choose their personal pathway. She has patience and empathy.

The Wise Woman is open to choose her method and vehicle for teaching. These vary from one individual to another. There are individuals with the Wise Woman archetype who are happy to engage in formal education within formal institutions. Some seek a lower profile and restrict their teaching to a small group or tribe. Others are content to use their archetypal Wise Woman energy to give guidance and advice only to their immediate friends and family. All methods to use their knowledge, wisdom and teaching skills are perfectly acceptable.

The degree to which a Wise Woman uses her abilities usually depends upon her circumstances, her confidence and her age. If the Wise Woman is the sole or major income earner, she is likely to seek a career within education. This may be as a primary or secondary school teacher, tertiary institution or community learning centre. If income is not the defining issue, the Wise Woman may be content to run a small business or participate in a local community support or spiritual group. Such involvement may be for personal development as well as for assisting others.

The energy and personality traits of the Wise Woman have always been with the individual. Often the Wise Woman is intent on inner transformation and personal growth. It may take a while to accept the knowledge and wisdom. It becomes a matter of confidence and trust in her ability. The more confident the Wise Woman is in her knowledge and advice, the more likely she is to take on a teaching role.

The other factor is age. In traditional terms, the Wise Woman of the tribe serves her apprenticeship at a young age. As she grows older and has more life experiences, she becomes known as the Sage or the Crone. This appears to be the case with most individuals with the Wise Woman archetype. They grow in wisdom, confidence and are more content to involve themselves in community and spiritual affairs as they mature and grow older.

Necessity, maturity and confidence are the essential reasons why the Wise Woman takes on the role of teacher. Inner knowledge and wisdom is a gift. The Wise Woman has this gift. The Wise Woman accepts the responsibilities that come with this gift when she is ready and on her terms. That is the nature of the Wise Woman growing into the Sage or Crone. That is, when they are ready, they are then willing to take on a serious leadership and teaching role.

❧ Motherhood and Family ❧

The Wise Woman has the knowledge and understanding to be a positive, nurturing and influential mother. In traditional terms, the Wise Woman holds the tribal wisdom and expertise with relationships, childbirth and the raising of children. Even with the development of a modern society, the energy is still the same. The individual with the Wise Woman archetype retains the wisdom and knowledge regarding relationships and children.

The energies of the Mother and the Wise Woman archetypes are similar in nature. Both have the caring and nurturing elements within the energy. Both have a strong attachment to the child energy and the protective nature to guard the child. Both archetypal energies encourage positive role modelling, effective teaching and the influential guiding of positive behaviours. When individuals with either of these archetypes tune in to their innate psychic abilities, they know and understand what is best for their child.

In some respect, the individual with the Wise Woman archetype is in a better position to develop a positive relationship with the child than the individual with the Mother archetype. This is because those with the Mother archetype tend to expend a lot of their Mother energy on other duties, such as partners, other children, household chores, financial management and other daily chores. The Mother energy carries with it a wide variety of expectation and personal involvement. The Wise Woman energy is more specific in nature. Therefore, it is easier for this individual to focus on the needs of the child without the hindrance of other distractions or duties.

The other aspect that assists the Wise Woman in dealing with and raising children is her broad range of knowledge and wisdom. The Wise Woman deals with all members of the tribe. She is exposed to a wide variety of issues that are brought to her by friends and acquaintances seeking advice. This gives her plenty of opportunity for learning and teaching. As we know, all children are different. The teacher, with extensive knowledge and wisdom is better equipped to deal with the diverse range of childhood challenges. This is the case with the Wise Woman

❧ Child Care ❧

The natural extension of the Wise Woman energy is to spread her influence into caring for all children, not just her own. The ability to understand and nurture children makes the Wise Woman the perfect candidate for working in child care. She has the knowledge and wisdom. She has the patience. She has the empathetic and protective nature.

The challenge, with which the Wise Woman may be confronted, is the legalities and management issues associated with child care organizations. As with many aspects of society, there are a vast array of rules and regulations that govern all manners of behaviours. The child care industry is no different. There are likely to be occasions when the knowledge and wisdom of the Wise Woman is confronted by an insistence of the authorities' rules and regulations.

The laws and regulations are determined by those in authority. Social history is rife with examples where the rights of children have been ignored or undermined. One has only to look at the stolen generation of Australian Aboriginal children. This policy is all the more galling as the Australian indigenous community is awash with Wise Woman energy. The Mothers and elders of the tribe always knew what was best for their children. Yet, many of these children were taken away to be raised by church and State authorities.

The Wise Woman has the knowledge and wisdom that understands the rights and needs of the individual child. These may not always fit in with the imposed requirements of a government department, business or child care centre.

It is important for the Wise Woman working in this area to be flexible and, at times, pragmatic. There are ways of working within a system and still promoting and enforcing sensible and righteous protocols. This is important for the Wise Women and the children in their care.

❧ Health and Healing ❧

Health is a central issue for the Wise Woman. The Wise Woman knows and understands what is in the best interests of her health and the health of others. There are individuals with the Wise Woman archetype working within the health system and on the fringe of the traditional health system.

As with child care, individuals working within the health system are restricted in certain ways. Even those on the fringe have to be aware of their role, their duty of care and how far they can push the boundaries of the governing laws and regulations.

With that understanding, there are a whole variety of opportunities that sit inside and outside of conventional health and medicine. There is employment as doctors, dentists and nurses. Knowledge is important in these positions. The Wise Woman has plenty of inner knowledge. She also has the ability and interest to succeed in study and learning. The Wise Woman excels at scholarly tasks. Working within the conventional medical system does have its advantages. However, for the Wise Woman, it is bound to have challenges. There are likely to be techniques, procedures and treatments that the Wise Woman knows to be ineffective and possibly harmful. This situation is one that tests the Wise Woman's morals and ethics.

The Wise Woman is perhaps more comfortable on the fringe of health and medicine. Here, there are ancient and proven treatments and techniques that are suited to the Wise Woman's inner knowledge and wisdom. Acupuncture, homeopathy, Bowen and Alexander techniques, massage and medicinal herbs are a few examples. Many of these were scorned and ridiculed by traditional Western medicine. Yet today, they all command respect and have a valued place in a variety of medical establishments.

Diet is another area where the expertise of the Wise Woman comes to the fore. This is essential work, especially given the poor quality of Western diets. These diets rely on take-away eating, packaged and processed meals and drinks laden with caffeine and sugar. Obesity and hyperactivity are on the rise and finally the health experts are pointing to the excesses in diets for this situation. Knowledge and wisdom has been buried by corporate profits and regulatory authorities. More than ever the knowledge and wisdom of the Wise Woman is crucial to inform those interested in personal health and diet.

✦ Psychology and Psychiatry ✦

The Wise Woman is likely to concern herself with all manner of healing. It is not only physical health that falls under her domain. There is also psychological and emotional well-being. Traditionally, the Wise Woman deals with all of these issues. It is her wisdom and understanding that brings others to them. It is also the fact that the Wise Woman has a particular interest in holistic healing.

Mental health and psychological well-being are issues to be dealt with in the establishment of a well-balanced individual. Therefore, the field of counselling, psychology and psychiatry is ideal for the Wise Woman.

This is especially the case in a modern society. Today there are a considerable number of pressures placed upon an individual. There is more to be concerned about than planning the next meal and where to sleep for the night. In most parts of the world, a more complex social structure has developed. Lives are full of responsibilities and opportunities. Expectations come from many sources. People are generally busy and involved. With this complexity comes stress and mental illness.

There are plenty of opportunities for the Wise Woman to involve herself in dealing with these complexities. It may be through formal training and education.

This is likely to lead to employment within the health portfolio with a large business entity or as a single practitioner. Formal training and a recognized qualification may encourage the Wise Woman to stay with further study or teach within the educational system.

Even without formal training and Qualifications, the Wise Woman may still find a place in psychology and mental health. It is within the archetypal energy of the Wise Woman where knowledge and wisdom is stored. She is likely to always attract others who require her advice and counselling. This is the nature of the Wise Woman energy.

⚜ Guidance or Relationship Counsellor ⚜

The field of guidance counselling and relationship management has expanded dramatically in recent years. Social conventions are changing rapidly. Relationships are undergoing a change in expectation. Today, life expectancy has increased. In this modern era, many individual are not committed to a life-long relationship. People fall in and out of relationships at a seemingly quick rate.

Dealing with relationships is another calling placed upon the Wise Woman. There are ample opportunities for the Wise Woman to act or find employment as a marriage guidance counsellor or relationship advisor. There are plenty of individuals looking to social media or dating services to begin and form a meaningful relationship. There are people of all ages looking for a change in their situation. All of these services come under the domain of the Wise Woman.

Once again the Wise Woman may be involved at a business level, a small group level or an individual level. Individual circumstances are likely to dictate where the Wise Woman develops and uses her knowledge, wisdom and communication skills. Confidence in her knowledge and ability also play an important role.

The key for the Wise Woman to understand is that she has the knowledge and wisdom. It is within her. Study, books, seminars, life experiences and the like enhances that knowledge and wisdom. The key is to be confident and trust in your ability.

Understand the wisdom within you. It has been there from a very young age. As you grow older and participate more in life, the wisdom reveals itself. Always remember, you are the Wise Woman.

✥ Workshop Facilitator ✥

One of the most effective ways of gathering the tribe is to hold workshops. This is where the Wise Woman plays an important role. Her role may be as a facilitator; gathering the tribe together, as a presenter or both.

The changing face of societies is seeing a lessening of the power and influence of traditional institutions. Religions, political parties, educational institutions, the press and other upholders of traditional social values have lost a great deal of their influence. Today, people are more mobile. They are not as committed to traditions and values. They use new technologies, especially those available with their mobile phone. They are influenced by social media and the connection with friends and acquaintances.

These changes have given more power to the individual. They are willing to participate in a variety of fresh experiences. This has given individual practitioners the opportunity to connect with others seeking new experiences and different ways of thinking. All of these changes enhance the role of the Wise Woman who is now in a strong position to gather people around them through workshops, seminars and gatherings. The threat of persecution and ridicule has diminished. As a facilitator or practitioner, the Wise Woman may speak the truth and assist others in the process.

Taking the role of workshop facilitator and presenter has benefits for both client and presenter. The more a presenter deals with others the more they learn. Each individual is different and have their personal set of personality traits, beliefs and challenges. Each group is different. It has a variety of energies within that group. Every workshop provides the opportunity for the presenter to learn more about the nature of their work and about human nature in general. For the Wise Woman, facilitating and presenting workshops are golden opportunities for more knowledge and wisdom.

𝔖ummary

You are the Wise Woman.

You have had wisdom and knowledge from a very young age.

Value that wisdom and knowledge.

Be confident in your knowledge and trust in your wisdom.

Assist those who come to you for advice.

You are the Wise Woman. You have been the Wise Woman all your life. You have an intimate knowledge of issues surrounding femininity, spirituality, health, children and relationships. You are the female authority of the tribe that surrounds you. As you grow older and have more life experiences, you become the Sage. Your wisdom is beyond reproach.

Have confidence in your knowledge and your wisdom. You have chosen this archetype to be the conduit for those who seek understanding, empowerment and transformation. Your family, friends and acquaintances recognize your abilities and that is why they come to you. Embrace your role as tribal advisor. Keep learning. Keep exploring. Keep the faith. You are the Wise Woman.

Treasure yourself and your attributes.

Remember

Your story is about;

- ❖ **how to harness your wisdom**
- ❖ **increase your knowledge**
- ❖ **use your psychic abilities with confidence**
- ❖ **assist those who come to you for advice**
- ❖ **maintain honesty and discretion**
- ❖ **establish and grow your status within the community**
- ❖ **experience personal growth to strengthen your link with the spiritual and the physical.**

Words of Wisdom
For Personal Use

Words of Wisdom
to Share

About the Author

Brian Dale is an author, archetype consultant, past life hypnotherapist and workshop facilitator. He is a retired primary school teacher and librarian.

Brian's giftedness in archetypes was an amazing discovery. In 2002, he trained as an archetype consultant at the Australian Institute of Caroline Myss. Archetypes are universal personifications, such as, Princess, King, Victim, Warrior, Rescuer and many more. We continually use archetypal energy in our daily lives. Brian realized he could assist people in the discovery and understanding of their true selves, how to operate in the various aspects of their lives and to bring change for their betterment and the benefit of others.

Archetypes give us an understanding of who we truly are. They are an incredible tool for self-empowerment. They allow us to change our lives when we move from the negative aspect of an archetype to the positive aspect of that archetype.

Brian's intuition and insightful observations have assisted many people to fully understand, empower and change themselves and their situation. He has given talks and lectures and facilitated archetype workshops overseas and throughout Australia.

With the passing of his daughter, Tahla, Brian has been inspired to investigate the Afterlife. This has taken him on a new and exciting pathway. He also trained as a QHHT practitioner. This is Delores Cannon's past life hypnotherapy technique.

"This is a new and stimulating journey. As a hypnotherapist, I am relishing each and every experience."

Brian is a published author and his stories for children have been used in standardized tests by both the Victorian and South Australian Education Departments. One of his greatest passions is drama and the performing arts. Brian is owner and teacher of Byron/Ballina Bright Lights Performance School.

Brian and his wife Robyn have been married for over forty years, have three wonderful children, Adam, Jade and Tahla and the most amazing grandchildren, Luca, Lilly and Isla (La La).